Wakefield

and my heart crumples like a coke can

They say those born overseas will always ache for the sky under which they were born. Ali Whitelock's particular bit of sky hovers above Scotland and spends most of its time obscured by clouds almost permanently pregnant with rain, hail, occasionally snow. Her first book, *poking seaweed with a stick and running away from the smell*, was published to critical acclaim in Australia and the UK. A few years later, after an abrupt life lesson, she stumbled upon Mary Oliver's *Tell me, what is it you plan to do with your one wild and precious life?* and took the decision to give up her spectacularly boring day job in order to write full-time. The book you are holding is her first poetry collection. Her poems have appeared in newspapers, magazines and journals in Australia, the UK and the USA, which Ali very much enjoys telling anyone who'll listen. She currently lives in Sydney.

praise for ali whitelock's
poking seaweed with a stick and running away from the smell

'Remarkably life affirming'—*Sydney Morning Herald*

'A hilarious, no-misery memoir'—*Scotsman*

'Candid and rhythmic . . . humour is her safeguard against the
terrible things she tells us'—*Sunday Herald* (Glasgow)

'Charmingly cynical'—*Scottish Review of Books*

'Joyous!'—Julie, Waterstones Lancaster

'Every once in a while you come across a story that will stay
with you long after the final page. This is one of those stories'
—*Chronicle*

'A funny, shocking, bittersweet account of growing up in
probably the most dysfunctional family in Scotland in the 70s'
—*Greenock Telegraph*

'Her book isn't a whinge-fest. Far from it. It's a funny account of
growing up in a Scottish family of battlers'—*Advocate*

'Pure nostalgia with funny bits—Ali Whitelock must be
Billy Connolly's comedy love child'—Laura Marney, author of
nobody loves a ginger baby, and *no wonder I take a drink*

'A raucous romp through a dysfunctional Scottish family.
Whitelock's storytelling is a wee delight'—Mandy Sayer,
author of *Dreamtime Alice* and *The Poet's Wife*

and my heart crumples like a coke can

ali whitelock

Wakefield
Press

Wakefield Press
16 Rose Street
Mile End
South Australia 5031
wakefieldpress.com.au

First published 2018

The following poems have been published before:
'the time it takes to boil an egg' in *Northwords Now*, Issue 32
'duty free fags' in *The Poets' Republic*, Issue 5
'if you write poetry but do not like conversation' in *Gutter*,
        The magazine of new Scottish writing, Issue 16
'there is no sound when it snows' in Red Room Company
        (as part of The Disappearing Project)
'eventually you will turn fifty' and 'ode to an ovary' in
        Beautiful Losers Magazine

Edited by Julia Beaven, Wakefield Press
Cover designed by Stacey Zass
Designed and typeset by Clinton Ellicott, Wakefield Press

ISBN 978 1 74305 534 2

A catalogue record for this
book is available from the
National Library of Australia

CORIOLE
McLAREN VALE

Wakefield Press thanks
Coriole Vineyards for
continued support

*To Thomas, whose wisdom saw beyond the insanity
and loved me still.*

contents

foreword by Mark Tredinnick   ix

a friend of mine with low self esteem   1
my dog has arthritis   3
fiona & the snow queen   5
eventually you will turn fifty   6
water's for fish   10
your friend said it was a love poem   12
what you must do you must keep your mouth shut   14
there is no sound when it snows   16
ode to an ovary   20
pakora for starters   22
diseased azaleas (azaleas morbus)   26
please do not pee in the sink   28
fridge poetry   31
mia council casa es tu council casa   33
the time it takes to boil an egg   36
let me eat cake and go quietly to seed   39
iona i came from far   41
the blue of god's fucking eyes   42
so she's not my friend and runs a fish & chip shop   45
o fair and gentle leek   47
my friend's vagina   49
in praise of the fairy cake   51
in kuntry where sun is never stopping shining   53
when the eagles have finished taking it easy   57
this is a prayer for the soul of my boy   58
single ply toilet paper   60

duty free fags   62
a lake full of fucking swans   64
on making a chocolate cake and not fucking up
    what's left of your relationship   67
and my heart crumples like a coke can   70
the reason your phone is not ringing   72
hector my hector   74
the shit we are in   76
dead man farting   79
if you write poetry but do not like conversation   82

end matters   84
acknowledgements   85

foreword

Ali Whitelock writes a poetry of excoriating tenderness. Her poems traffic a profane divination of a self—her own, although she could be any one of us at all. They travel a constellation of worlds—in particular a childhood country (Scotland) configured as a blighted paradise, and a found place (suburban Australia and more latterly a bushy 'burb by the beach), which she writes of as if it were an almost good-enough marriage, an exile begrudgingly becoming a home.

Whitelock's refusal of traditional forms, of punctuation and capitalisation, makes of her prosy lyric rants an utterance that stands naked yet somehow modest, laughing not unkindly at herself and all of us and forgiving everything but cant. One is stripped and disabused by these poems— which are the Bardic speakings, irreverent sermons on no one's mount, of a poet much more in love with poetry and its clarifying, soul-making project than she ever could be with her own.

You will meet Whitelock's dog here and love him and mourn for his passing. You will make a chocolate cake and fuck up what's left of your relationship. You will start again. And again. You will grow old and learn to love it better than you thought you could love anything or anyone. You will join her too late beside her violent but deeply human father's hospital bed. You will know her friend's vagina. You will disdain but come grudgingly to admire the tolerance, the low expectations and cheap conversation of contemporary Australia. You will make friends with the man you shied from at first as if he were a terrorist, but who turns out to be lost like all of us, only wiser than fuck.

There is room for failure in the sound world Whitelock makes here, there is room for falling way short; but there is no time for cliché, delusion, pomp or bastardry.

Whitelock is Bukowski with a Glaswegian accent and a nicer wardrobe. Ali Whitelock is Sharon Olds with better manners, learned on the wrong side of the tracks, with dignity mastered as a survival technique. Hers is a humanity distilled from loss and violence she has survived and transfigured into kindness. She swears like an angel and sings up heaven like a drunk; she is as sober as the last light of day.

These are performance poems performed draft after slow draft very quietly on paper. These are voicings distinct as geographies, proud as selves; they are, these unstinting scrutinies, these unchurched hymns, as everyday as washing up, as necessary as shopping, as bracing as a winter walk along a northern shore, as painful as cancer, as intoxicating as one drink too many, as bracing as failure, as uplifting as coming through. These poems wake you. They are conversations with a better best friend than you ever had. One who lets you do all the talking and then picks up the cheque.

Poems should be tender and slender and lonely, said Basho, and Whitelock's are. Way wordier than Basho would have liked, but achieving a similar silence on the page and in the reader's coke can heart—a silence in which wisdom may begin to arise, and if it does, you will have won it as hard as she has.

Ali Whitelock takes herself apart here and puts us all back together; she disassembles her memories and hopes and delights, her places, her father, all of us in our imperfections and banalities; and she makes of herself and all of us a new and possible start.

These are poems of deep integrity—no gap at all between the inner thought and the outer utterance. But they only seem as though they've come easily to mind and spoken themselves in a rush. These are improvisations rehearsed and performed as if they hardly cared for how they sounded at all. Alison Whitelock attends very closely to language that seems casual, but is carefully fashioned, syllable by spoken syllable, until it is the kind of deeply human one that only rarely gets to be, and only after a lot of practice. You'll find a voice here so distinctive it could be your own. Whitelock's informality is an act of deep humanity and self-abnegation and care, a refusal to let anyone else live her life or shape her being in it. These are vernacular, elegant rants. They keen and they yearn and they warn and they thank the stars for not falling more often than they do. These poems, trying not to be poems at all, are acts of love and defiant triumphs of order over disorder, Hurrahs that cry down all disarray.

Mark Tredinnick, 2018
winner of the Montreal International Poetry Prize and the author of *The Lyre Bird & Other Poems*, *Bluewren Cantos*, *Australia's Wild Weather*, *Fire Diary*, *The Blue Plateau* and *The Little Red Writing Book*

a friend of mine with low self esteem

it is a very high-brow bookstore
i like the books in there. they also have penguin
tote bags and scrabble mugs and badges
you can buy which say i read books and you can pin
these badges to your lapel so when you are not reading
a book people will know that you do
they have a sign at the front door that says
you must leave your bag at the counter
and this is because they are worried you might
steal a book from them
the poetry books are upstairs the red carpet
that leads you there is not very worn the staff
in the bookstore do not say hello to you
or be nice to you because they are very
intellectual only they cannot find a job doing
an intellectual thing and so they must scan barcodes
and put aside the books that have been ordered in
then they must ring up the customers to tell them
their books are ready for collection
the other thing they must do is instruct
people to swipe or tap or insert and sometimes
there is cash and they must count it at the end of the night.
Because they have degrees and phds they cannot
do anything with they are also quite rude because
their self esteem is quite low
a friend of mine has low self esteem too
she read a book about it and told me there
is an app you can download if you have an iPhone 6

i went to the high-brow bookstore
to buy the book when you are looking
for a book in the high-brow bookstore
you can ask the scary lady at the computer
to check if they have it in stock i always
look on the shelves first because i do not want
to disturb the scary lady at the computer who always
looks like she is doing very important work
sometimes the work she is doing is so important
she cannot look up from the keys to let you know
she can see you standing there waiting
the book i wanted was not on the shelf
so i went to the scary lady at the computer and waited.
The scary lady had lots of things to attend
to before she could look up and see me standing
at the counter and when she did i asked her
if she could check to see if they had a copy of the book
the scary lady at the computer exhaled and said
could i just wait because now she had to change
screens then she did a lot of key tapping
and more of the exhaling thing then she said sorry
they didn't have it and went back to her very important
things again
and even though she said she was sorry
she didn't really sound sorry because
when you are an intellectual sometimes
you do not have time to sound sorry.
Before i left i asked her if she could suggest
another book that might be similar *'oh i don't read
books like that,'* she said. Too loudly
in my opinion.

my dog has arthritis

my dog has arthritis he is the size of a small horse
it is a lot of weight for him to carry
i give him the best care i can. Expensive
visits to the vet injections here fleecy
winter coats there buy him fish oils when they are on special
at coles
someone not a friend just someone told me the best quality
fish oils are from the heath food store that they keep them
in a locked cupboard and the bottles do not display
the price and this makes me feel very uncomfortable
the last fish oils i bought from coles were seven dollars
for four hundred capsules i give my dog eighteen
each day that is six at breakfast six at lunch
and six at dinner i met a woman on the beach
she was an ICU nurse once at the glasgow royal infirmary
where my sort-of-sister-in-law lies right now she is forty
has had a massive heart attack is in an induced
hypothermic coma and the pain of this knowing
kills me a little more with every day. The nurse notices
my dog's limp i tell her he has arthritis
that i give him fish oil i tell her about the four hundred
capsules for seven dollars and she agrees it is a good price
then i hear myself tell her i give him nine
at breakfast nine at lunch and nine at dinner
as if real life events are not already
bad enough like that time the stag leapt
from the cliff and landed on the beach dead, only
it wasn't a stag it was a fawn and the ICU nurse

and i talked of that stag each time we met told passersby
of its size measured out the crater its dead body
had left in the sand she said her dog fed at its throat
i said my dog devoured its brains and rolled in the smell
of it long after it had been removed by the council
with a tractor.

fiona & the snow queen

they ask how she is and i tell them:
today she took two steps ate a half tub of
    yoghurt sang prince songs out of tune said thank
christ that's not me when the curdling screams rang
    out from the bed next door
and these things don't sound like much
    but if you knew how her heart broke how it snapped
in two how we cried that many tears we could've filled
    a burn. Then the snow queen came and cooled her
till now she is frozen and he spends nights with her
    and days feeds her liquidised lunches massages
her scalp plays the remix version of one of their songs
    and even she in her dreamlike state concludes
it is utter shite and i know he does not want to talk about
    what might happen next whether the frosts of her winter
will thaw and the first green shoots of her spring
    reappear. He says he will sing to her.
He is musical i am not. All i can do is record in words
    to say what has happened
though the end is not clear yet.

eventually you will turn fifty

and this will be the day you lose your mind.
You will produce honey and certain insects
will be attracted to you
you will put on a dab of hollywood red lipstick
this will be the same colour you discovered
when you were ten in the cardboard mushroom
carton that doubled as your mother's make-up box
and when you emerged from the bathroom wearing
the lipstick your father told you you looked like a fucking
whore and it will surprise you that actually
he was wrong
you will put on a black frock which never
used to but now clings to the rolls you seem
to have developed overnight. These rolls
will make you appear more womanly and you will not mind
    this one bit
you will start to take more time over your hair
buy a pair of earrings in the jewellery shop
that is closing down they will match your lipstick
and you will look beautiful because your hair
will fall over one eye and this will make you look sultry
you will even consider putting on the MAC eyeshadow
you bought seven years ago and never opened
it may still be good. A man you do not know
will tell you your earrings make the green
of your eyes look very nice and you will laugh
and look away as though you are shy though
you will hope the lens of his camera is still
upon you

you will have spent twenty years with the same partner
this partner will love you more and better than anyone
ever could including your own mother who loves you
	very much
eventually your earrings and lipstick will cause your partner
substantial discomfort though he will not say anything
about it because he will know that turning
fifty sometimes means that things might change
and he will know that all he can do is wait to see if anything
is still standing once the high pressure
system has moved through and although he is not a buddhist
he will accept the river of life will sometimes
burst its banks that water will rise in kitchens
and the insurers will need to be called in to assess the damage
to the european appliances and you will know something
inside you is dying now that the tub of fresh double cream
that has sat happily at three degrees in the refrigerator
of your life is now on the turn. You will meet a man
you did not expect to meet you will want to spend
many nights with him you will make up many excuses
as to why you are coming home late you will ask your
	girlfriend
who is also very good at lying to join you in your dreich den
of dishonesty and she will agree to act as your alibi
should your partner of twenty years decide to call her one
	night to confirm you are with her.
On the evenings you are not home your partner
of twenty years will eat dinner on his own
and he will cling wrap yours so when you come home
he can microwave it for you so you can have a hot meal
he will know that things are now very different
and he will know exactly what is different

but he will not say anything about it because
he will not want to make you feel you cannot behave
in the way you find you suddenly need to behave
he will notice you are now shaving your legs
having your bikini line waxed and sometimes
your nails painted fire engine red and he will not believe
the outrageous lies you are telling him
but he will not call you on them and this will
make you think you are getting away with them
and even though he is not a buddhist he will
not show you any rage rather he will love
you all the more because he will understand
that what you need right now is love
and one morning when you will have stuffed
your liver so full of your own lies that it sits
swollen like that of a french goose
he will ask you gently if you want to talk about
what's going on and still you will tell him everything
is fine and keep on with your lies till you are now choking
on them
eventually you will be home for dinner less and less
and you will lie to him more and more
and one night you will send him a text saying
you will be back later than usual maybe even the next day
and your lie for this one will be very original and completely
unbelievable but you are now so addicted
to your lies like a kid on nothing but smarties and mars bars
and tob-le-fucking-rones that you just keep right on
shovelling your refined sugar onto the fire of your truth
and your partner of twenty years will text you back simply
saying 'OK' 'cause he knows you need to go through what

you need to go through and he will eat dinner alone
that night along with all the other nights and he will wash
the dishes and watch the evening news and he will miss
that you are not there shouting at the telly when the liberals
come on and he will put the hot water bottle on your side
of the bed and cling wrap your dinner because
he understands the importance of a warm bed
and a hot meal when you finally come home.

water's for fish

as cliché as it may sound i always
imagined i'd get the call in the middle
of the night the one that would announce
that you were dead or at the very least
be dying i'd be bleary eyed would thank
the caller and hang up grateful
that i am safe my seventeen thousand
kilometres away and geographically exempt
from delivering your eulogy from shaking
hands with those i have no wish to shake
hands with i would not have to be seen
to weep nor to wonder at the choice
of photograph someone else has chosen
for your order of service for these
are the things that happen when you're gone too long
weirdly i was coming back to visit you mum
you'd been unwell minor kidney failure
for fuckssake how many years have we been asking
you to drink water? Water's for fish you'd say
—not so smart now are you? Then you made
this miraculous recovery too late i'd already
booked my ticket to come and sit at your bedside
to hold your hand to keep you company on your descent
into complete renal failure so my daughterly
dash would become a holiday instead, the last
of which was too long ago though i still
recall the sweetness of the sangria the paellas
filled with prawns and crabs and bits of lobster i scraped
to the side of my plate and i know a holiday

in glasgow's not for everyone
sure we don't get paella and we don't
get crabs but we do get fish and chips
and deep-fried mars bars and unending
poetry nights that run the length of argyle street
and around the corner into shipbank lane
so i got onto google and i planned
i booked myself on writers' groups on open mics
circled poetry readings i'd attend i'd hop across
to paris maybe berlin fuck it why not barcelona?
but a quick drop in to see you father revealed
you were a sliver of yourself
a flaked almond of a man
a fragment
like someone took a photocopy
of you reduced it to A5 printed it in grey scale
'you look like shit,' i told you, embraced you
'i know,' you mouthed back. I didn't know
you could no longer speak that your teeth no longer
fitted you that you could barely swallow
and no one knew not even margo the annoying
nutritionist who did the home visits
that very soon (in exactly nine days as it
turns out) i would not be hopping across
to paris maybe berlin fuck it why not barcelona
but would be delivering your eulogy written by my sister
and scheduled to be read somewhere between
the eagles *taking it easy* and john denver *filling*
up our senses like sleepy blue oceans and i am unsure
i will make it past the most perfect and excruciating
first line. 'He was no saint our father but he used to say
he looked like roger moore.'

your friend said it was a love poem

a thousand and thirty-seven days ago
somewhere between leaving home and arriving
at the david jones department store i lost my moral
compass. When i left home that morning i was married,
dependable. I ironed underpants tablecloths
kept the fridge full dog walked plants watered.
I retrieved odd socks from behind the washing machine,
spread butter, spooned jam to the corners
of toast even though the stickiness on my fingers
drove me up the fucking wall i used to be good.
But the pull of your magnetic field was so strong you see
and you were nothing to look at—bald head broken
specs jeans from kmart, obsessive compulsive—that's one way
of putting it. But light shone from you and i was flooded
by it. One night i wrote you an email and you replied
each of your lines perfectly poised between mine till your
response became a poem in itself and i took this as proof
that you were The One. The truth is a thousand and thirty-
seven days ago you'd have moved the heaven, the earth,
climbed mountains crossed deserts weathered storms
to hold my hand to drink from my cup, to breathe
me in. It was winter then. I wrapped you in my coat.
Wrote a poem about you. You showed it to your friend
which surprised me. Your friend told you it was a love
poem which i suppose it was though i'd never
have used the L word. Not out loud. Not around you.
The truth is i spent countless nights with you
on your japanese futon and i'd have slept

on a bed of nails to be with you. The mornings—
room barely lit with filtered dawn and guilt i'd rise, linger,
lean my ear in against your breath before showering
away my lies and returning home the truth is i fell
in love with you the worst was the pleasure
you took in telling me you didn't feel the same
for months i leaked pain lost sleep survived
on one chewing gum a day imagined how cancer
might feel the therapist had seen it all before—a thousand
times apparently—in women my age with no children
go on then rub it in at least i'd had the presence
of mind to ask about diseases you said
you had none backed it up with a printout
of your latest blood results you kept in a folder
marked 'bloods' which i didn't find strange.
The truth is the therapist told me it would
take eighteen months for the feelings to subside
and i could barely manage eighteen minutes
without you i checked my phone a thousand
times a day analysed the syllables in every email
you'd ever sent listened to radiohead watched *eternal*
sunshine of the spotless mind changed therapist.
Months later—okay so eighteen—i woke and found myself
in the final rinse in the washing machine
of my discontent and the world that entered
my mouth tasted faintly of honey then the sunflowers
grew and the bees came back and pollen blew free
in the warmth of the wind.

what you must do
you must keep your mouth shut

if you want to you can tape it shut
with the snoring tape—he keeps it on the side of his bed.
Sometimes
it rolls off onto the carpet
the cat hair sticks to it because
what you must understand
is how you feel is not how others
feel. The important
thing you must do is not say how you feel
if you say how you feel he will roll his eyes and sometimes
after the eye rolling
there will be a sigh and what that means is you must not say
that thing again. Eventually
you will get to know the things that make the eyes roll and
the chest sigh and you will stop saying
them. If you hold a hermit crab shell to your ear
you can hear a rushing
and this rushing is the sound
of everything and the sound of nothing
and one morning when you drive
him to the station
he may ask you how you are feeling
and what you must do is you must
say you slept well the breakfast
was nice and it is very hot today
another time when you will pick him up from the station
he may ask you what's wrong

and what you must
do is not say anything
about what is wrong with
you. The other
thing you can do
is hold the hermit
crab shell up to
his ear and he will
hear the sound
of everything
and the sound
of nothing
then there
will be the
rolling and the sighing
and what that
means is if
you have to feel
that way—feel
that way
quietly.

there is no sound when it snows

like when you pull your tam o'shanter
down over your ears and i know this muffled
silence so well it is there always
in the forest at the end of our road
where conifer boughs layered with thick snow sway
like fat babies just fed, their heads
lolling on the brink of nodding off and the train
to london whizzes past twice a day punctuating
the silence with two giant exclamation
marks triggering tremors causing snow
to loosen and waltz from boughs with a whispering swoosh
and there were times i was on that train
mum would drop me at the station in the village
then race back through the forest
to wave as my train sped past and as the forest
approached i'd wave through the window
though the train went so fast i could never
quite see her—but i knew that she was there.
The air is iced and sharp here and i breathe
it willingly stick my tongue in the air
catch snowflakes that flit i swallow
their flesh drink down their blood
till i am the snowflake the snowflake is me.
I lived here once. In this icy silence.
The place i live now is hot and there are days
i could weep for the boughs of my forest
and the north wind that gusts and near blows
the toorie off my glengarry this hot place i live is australia

the land is dry and cracked here
much like the skin on the heels of my feet
that were never like that when i lived in scotland
i've got my father's feet they say heels
that need softening in the bath for a fortnight
before you could even begin to take the cheese
grater to them and only then will the thick skin
come away crumbly like the mature scottish
cheddar i've never enough money to buy in the supermarket
things have changed since i came to this hot
place i've forgotten a lot about scotland
sure that's what i came here for in the first
place but i have my reminders all around
me now indeed as i lay here on my bed
on this hot january afternoon wilting
from the searing heat and not a breath
of air to be had my dog-eared copy of antonia
fraser's *mary queen of scots* jams my sash
window open since the cord of the sash snapped
and sent the upper case hurtling to the sill
like the guillotines that have taken the french
heads off more people than i care to remember
and i have my postcard on the wall
the one of the highland cow my brother
sent me from his camping trip on skye—
'come back ali' it reads 'before you forget
how good this air truly tastes' and i read
that card daily and it too is dog-eared
for i peel it from the wall each morning
and stick it back with the same lump of blu
tac i've been using for the last as many years

17

i can't move in this heat
all i can do is lie here on my now damp cotton
sheets damp from the sweat i've been leaking
as hot winds torch and burnt dust swirls forcing
locals into bars with promises of half price
cocktails served in coconut shells at times
of day not made for drinking
i moved into this weatherboard cottage
with hardly a thing it was the first place
i'd lived in australia with a garden—i should
say yard—they call gardens yards down here
yards make me think of barbed wire fences
broken concrete slabs and gnashing
guard dogs on choke chains that near sever
their windpipes rushing strangers that come too close
the day i moved in i sat in my new garden
overgrown with something green and curly
—chokoes the neighbour advised—whatever
the fuck chokoes are i looked them up 'native
to mexico though particularly easy to grow
in the australian *yard*' and this house
came with a fish pond baking in full sun
naked of algae and the loneliest most bored looking
goldfish i have ever seen he barely moves
does not dart nor scoot unlike the darting
scooting goldfish of my youth won at fairgrounds
knocking the heads off clowns with a coconut
i call this goldfish gordon for no other
reason than it starts with a g
sometimes i sit under my choko vine
and stare at him. Once in a while he swims

half-heartedly from one end of his blistering
pond to the other humiliated by mosquitoes
landing on fairy feet pricking the surface
of his pond there was a time he must have eaten them—
i don't see him so much as place his lips
to the surface now all he does is hang
with all the weight of the depressed
man who can barely lift his head
off the pillow and i get to thinking
all this goldfish has probably ever
known is life in this simmering pond
but me i've known something different
i've seen my frosted breath hang in the stillest
of air and my lips have kissed the chill
of snow that brings a silence money
couldn't buy you so i'll lie here
on my damp sheets a wee while longer
and i'll dream of scotland and mary
queen of scots and two-man tents on skye
where toories are taken in gale-force winds
and goldfish are not boiled alive in some scalding
pond
sure this hot country is no place for a goldfish
this hot country is no place for me.

ode to an ovary

your belly protruded me invaded I could not breathe you could
have held it in you chose not to it's natural you think to have it
stick out like demi moore on the front cover of that magazine
you give a photographer too much money to shoot you and your
bump naked you post the pictures on the net you get no hits
nobody wants to look at you and your bump naked 'cept maybe
your adoring husband who works in finance so you can drive a
mercedes your alabaster breasts are full of low-fat milk you go
to pilates on wednesdays yoga on tuesdays you read buddhism
for busy mothers smile serenely at waitresses wipe your decaf
latte moustache with the lavender scented hanky you bought
at the overpriced french shop on the corner you invite your
friends around you feed them cassoulet and coq au vin from a
can you are trying for more babies don't have to think about
IVF your friend is sad she wanted three only managed two poor
thing distraught. I don't fucking care. You buy blue cheeses
from france you eat them with fennel crackers you drink non-
alcoholic sparkling semillon on sunday afternoons after tennis
while the calcium is being leeched from my fucking bones
and my worn-out body flushes every two fucking minutes your
ovaries are not borderline malignant your uterus is intact not
sliced from you by men in blue scrubs with plastic bags on
their shoes yours functions perfectly in its dark red silence a
venus flytrap snapping at the eggs your athletic and successful
husband in finance will fertilise for you with a hole in fucking
one you don't have to worry he won't get a hard-on while
you're ovulating at 6pm on a tuesday eleven days after your
last period you feel sorry for your forty-something husbandless

girlfriends asking gay men to masturbate into tumblers then squirting the contents into their vaginas they keep their legs high in the air it makes it stick don't you know they heard it on oprah you have more estrogen than you deserve your fallopian tubes are fresh and slender your eggs slide effortlessly from your non-stick teflon ovaries every twenty-eight fucking days you could put the kettle on for them you have one baby you want two you should live in china or get a dog you're not demi fucking moore.

pakora for starters

i stop
at the nurses' station on the way in ask male nurse
kevin about your hallucinations since they dropped
your tramadol from sixteen to one a day
he picks up your chart scrunches his eyes
like he's two thirds blind and his nose
scrunches in unison like it doesn't have a fucking
mind of its own then he puts on his specs
holds the clipboard at arm's length attempts
to decipher the clinician's scrawl the casual
jottings-down the soulless recordings
the matter-of-fucking-fact facts of your fluids
in and solids out your thin scotch broth and bland
poached fish your watered down custard
and two fruits in syrup, 'nothing about
the hallucinations,' kevin says still trying to decode
the manic scribble that looked like a fly
with parkinsons just crash landed on the page
and tried to crawl to safety but died on the fucking way,
'but it looks like they're going to test him
for . . . now let me see . . .' he said, focusing intently
like a boy scout without matches trying to start
a fire in the woods with a magnifying glass
a ray of sun and a pile of dried up leaves
and eventually the first orange lick of a flame
appeared and the embers of stunned consonants and vowels
crackled back into existence and kevin
strung them together reading them out loud

like he'd just learnt to read that morning,
'm-m-m-m—o-t-o-r . . .' he drawled like he'd just
had a fucking stroke, 'n-n-n-n—e-e-e—u,' he continued
on—very fucking painfully—'r-o-o-o-o—n-e . . . *aaahhhh!*
   motor neurone!'
he squealed proudly like the final piece of sky
in a jigsaw entirely of sky was just dropped
into place then he slumped back into his chair
mopped up beads of sweat that had pooled
in the worry lines of his brow exhaled
in that relieved way when you finally get the skelf
out of your finger or remember the capital of norway
in the geography quiz in front of the entire fucking school
and kevin was that happy with his achievement
like he'd just won the duke of fucking edinburgh
award that i felt happy too i mean it wasn't
like the notes said they were testing my father
for pancreatic cancer or emphysema or fucking
ebola and 'motor neurone' sounded so innocent—
so harmless like something merely went wrong
with one of the neurones in my father's motor
and furthermore when kevin said motor neurone out loud
i did not hear death bells peal nor angels
cry proof indeed that whatever was wrong with my father
could not possibly be as bad as we'd feared
i hummed a wee tune
happy on my way in to the four man ward
and the telly blared in the corner rangers
thrashing celtic and you'd be pleased catholics
crushed like muscatels and yet you married one
converted to catholicism yourself made promises

you had no intention of keeping before
a god you did not believe in and i held up the new fangled
tube of condensed milk i got you from asda
it used to come in tins do you remember?
you used to spread it thick on bread with butter
and i understand that now—it is something about
the sweetness and creaminess that comforts
i removed my coat and hat laid them down
on your well tucked-in feet if they know anything
here it is hospital corners it was a night
for gloves and scarves and fake fur-lined boots
and new found lightness and i will order
the saag aloo on the way home with plain boiled
rice and two vegetable pakoras with the pink
minty sauce and you will continue seeing things
the rest of us cannot see. I took my seat by your side
talked to you of weather of emmerdale farm of coro-
-fucking-nation street and you asked if i could
see them—the diamonds spilling in the air right
there in front of you and you reached out and plucked
one pressed it into my palm, 'for you,' you whispered
then you snatched some more held them tight to your chest
beckoned me closer and i leaned in only
when you opened your palm your hand lay empty
and your green baffled eyes searched frantically
between your fingers in the cuffs of your pajamas in the holes
of your cellulose blanket and your face turned
the colour of disbelief like you'd just seen
god in the pub nursing a pint only
by the time your pals got there god was gone and everyone
thought you were losing your mind

then your eyes turned to the bare white wall across
from your bed, 'can you see it?' you whispered pointing
at the slick ocean liner carving her way through
a black swollen sea great puffs of smoke spewing
from her freshly painted funnel, 'the *titanic!*' you gasped
and your finger tracked her voyage across the bare white wall
and despite my conversation with kevin i no longer
felt happy and light i now feared the iceberg
up ahead i glanced frantically in the corners
of the four man ward for life jackets and flares
a hammer to please break glass in case
of emergency i screamed to my imaginary captain
to man the lifeboats! The sick and dying first! For fuckssake
sauve-qui-peut! and my ocean rose and fell around
me i gagged into the sick bag of my mind as hundred
foot waves battered my bow and shocks of post vomit
hair plastered my cheeks and i asked you where your liner
was headed. 'I don't know,' you whispered,
'but she's headed there fast.'

diseased azaleas (*azaleas morbus*)

australia i have lost
something of myself
in your cleared bush
your so-called suburbs
masquerading as civilisation
with six lanes of aesthetically
bereft hot roads lined
with beige villas obligatory
holden commodores parked
proudly on front lawns
in full view of lounge room
windows no topiary
as centrepieces for these
gardens no water fountains
no bird baths
no perfectly pruned
willows that might
weep for cooler days
but power cables
that dangle sloppily
crisscrossing main roads
like a home-sweet-fucking-
home cross-stitch gone
wrong i walk my dog
around these pavement-less
streets he craps on hot
lawns where sprinklers
sprinkle boredom where

incongruent water taps rise like
periscopes from blow-torched
grass where diseased azaleas
and brown shrubs that once
passed for french lavender
reside:

METHOD

1. take one piece of perfectly good bush
2. bulldoze
3. remove soul in its entirety
4. displace original inhabitants
5. build ugliest dwellings imaginable
6. use most inferior building materials available
7. build shops too far away
8. do not provide public transport
9. force them into their cars
10. call these too far away shops shopping villages

these un-beating hearts
of franchised subways
and hair salons with the shittiest
names like headquarters
and fringe benefits and why don't
you just curl up and fucking
die and refrigerated counters
filled with chicken parts
and humble sausages tortured
into believing they are more
than they really are.

please do not pee in the sink

in the cafe with coffee cups for lampshades
and the sign that says please do not pee
in the sink we take an outside table
we have been coming here for years. We consider
this table to be ours. Today there is an unexpected
madman at the table next to us he is leaping
to his feet every five minutes kneeling
in the middle of the footpath and praying
to allah
i tell my husband i think we should go
that the praying man in the unfashionable
blouson is—i will confess—scaring
me a little my husband tells me i'm being
ridiculous like four years ago when the spider
lay in wait for me in the toilet
and he had to remove it before
i could pee and every time since i have gone
i take a torch scan the front and back of the door the inside
of the toilet-roll tubes and under the wicker
basket where i keep the earth choice toilet
cleanser and the eco friendly air freshener
we always bring our dog to this cafe
the internet tells us muslims
do not like dogs they make their prayers
impure it is their version of us peeing
in the sink our coffees have no sooner
arrived than the unexpected madman
is down on his knees again and i leak involuntary

squeals like air escaping from the mouth
of an over-inflated balloon and my imagination
made fertile by too frequent watering convinces me
his unfashionable blouson is packed with explosives
and post-detonation there'll be skimmed cappuccino
froth and body parts scattered the length of glebe point road.
In all the years we've been coming
here the daily special has never changed something
about fettucini in a mushroom sauce with pesto
and a hint of dijon—not dijon *mustard*—just dijon
as though the chef might wear a french beret
and cycle to work with a string of onions hanging
off the handlebars of his bicyclette next time
we came to the cafe the unexpected madman
was there and the time after that and the time after that
and every five minutes he'd be down on his knees.
Months passed like this.
Days drifted.
We kept coming.
He kept praying.
Nothing exploded.
Eventually we came to enjoy watching mothers
with strollers wide berth him and dog walkers
drag reluctant puppies to the other side of the road
then one day he rose made eye contact pointed
at our dog said 'yoouurr dog verry beeg'
we nodded.
He smiled.
Next time we came he offered his hand we shook
it bought him coffee shared our fags
months passed like this.

Days drifted.
Sometimes when i'd come alone he'd ask—'verr is hussbant?'
i'd tell him he's at work
buy him a coffee he'd smile point at hector
'yourrr dog verry beeg'
more months passed like this.
More days drifted.
One day he tells me he is looking
forrr job asks me for two bucks i give him five in his country
he is accountant his english skills are poor i worry
how he will manage i've taken to minding
his stuff while he's down on his knees i make sure
no one touches his unfashionable
blouson his lighter his fags his yale lock key yesterday
when i arrived he wasn't there
i looked up glebe point road saw him in the distance
walking towards the cafe hair combed, high-vis vest
working boots he stopped at my table pressed a crumpled
five dollar note into my palm cupped
his hands warmly around mine 'forrr yoouu'
he said 'i hefffff job now' and he smiled
his charming middle eastern smile pointed
at hector 'yoouurr dog verry beeg' he said.
I couldn't have agreed more.

fridge poetry

then there was the bangle on your table
when you came back from hong kong
left behind by one of the others
i assumed, the chinese one perhaps
who makes the best szechuan prawns in balmain
and i can barely boil an egg.
And on my birthday
you bought me fridge poetry magnets
and a card which, when opened,
burped and the message inside read:
happy burp-day
you thought i didn't laugh 'cause i didn't get it.
That same day i told you i didn't want to see you again.
Not because of the card
there were other things—much worse than the card
you looked surprised
your shoulders slumped
you arranged your best devastated frown
hung your head the way a dog might do when
there are no more bones oh ali
you said and from a certain angle
i thought you may actually have meant it
though you'd been in film for years
you knew how to make fiction appear
real
i drove twenty-one kilometres that day
to a town i did not know dropped
the bangle and the burp card in a

wheelie bin outside a chicken shop
selling spicy wing dings medium chips
cans of schweppes and sometimes
in my lighter moments i think back—imagine
the owner of that bin
opening the lid and the burps
ringing out far across the land.
The fridge poetry magnets went in
that bin too though not until i'd stuck
cunt
fuckwit
arsehole
on my refrigerator door.

mia council casa es tu council casa

i live out of sydney these days it is close
to the beach though we are not wealthy.
Some days there are whales other days dolphins
occasional jellies and never dead babies i like visiting
the art gallery in the city it takes me one hour
to drive there i park at the expensive
multi-storey it is a $10 flat rate on a sunday
after parking i cut through hyde park past the statue
of robert burns standing alone and too far away
from scotland we are both foreigners here of the acceptable
kind i like the location of the gift shop
it is right next to the entry which is also the exit
i always go to the gift shop first, they have handbags
made of unshaved cow and earrings like hot air balloons
and a dimly lit section at the back with mysterious
art books in thick polythene covers the thickness
of the polythene indicates their seriousness
and the price and there is an arsehole in there wearing
jesus sandals though he bears no resemblance
to jesus and the arsehole says to a random woman
(who turns out to be an arsehole too) he took
a holiday in paris once on the left bank some
thirty years back when it really was something
and if hitler were alive today this whole thing
with the syrian refugees would not be happening
and the female arsehole agrees then the jesus
sandalled arsehole says what's going on over
there is nothing but a european invasion

and the subject of the little boy's body on bodrum
beach comes up and i have been there on holidays
some thirty years back when it really was something
the hotel was right next door to the doctor's surgery
bent black-clad women came daily clacked rosary
beads on milk crates in full view of fat tourists
bathing topless on hotel lounges ordering
chips and cokes they did not need from kadir
the turkish waiter who brought me proper chai
in a glass and taught me how to say
'tomorrow i am going to instanbul'.
After the little boy's body got washed
up on the sand australia offered synthetic
duvets fake chai lattes and empty promises
to twelve thousand of the five million
in camps who cry themselves to sleep at night
and i have calculated this on my iPhone and it works
out to be a teardrop in the ocean to the closest
decimal point australia i have offered
more hope to more cockatoos more safety
to kookaburras more gum leaves to koalas
than the crumbs you are flicking
from your all-you-can-eat buffet
it is time to feed the birds australia
tuppence a fucking bag sure what does it cost
to pipe in a haggis share some tatties and neeps
raise a glass to their health mia council
casa es tu council casa australia the world's
eyes are rolling in your general direction
and right now you look like some kind of jesus
sandalled arsehole sitting on the veranda

of your ocean front property with your deep pockets
and short arms pretending you don't even know
it's your turn to buy the next round at the bar.

the time it takes to boil an egg

the last taste
in your mouth would
have been that of terror
as strangers in white coats and non-slip shoes
punched you hard in the fucking
chest while i wandered the house of fraser
smearing creamy tracks of hot plum and shocking
coral on the thin underside of my forearm
at the counter with the french sounding
name and when my phone rang i heard the words
alright—as though florence nightingale herself
had said them—and i raced like some kind
of lipstick coated crazy fuckwit from the house
of fraser to the car i cannot find in the car park
i am sure i have parked in and i queue
the excruciating twelve seconds
for the man in front to pay i smash my credit
card in the slot insert my ticket at the boom
am urged by electronic ticker tape to please drive
carefully and have a nice day please—fucking—spare
me the clichés as i race down the antiseptic hall
past the hand sanitiser cover your mouth when coughing
and have you had your flu shot this year i hurtle
towards the nurses' station with its limp carnations
and male nurse kevin plastic aproned stewing tea
and arranging supermarket custard creams
for the three o'clock highlight okay
so you called him a poof that time but still

he took your vitals checked your stools updated
your charts and points now on my arrival
to the side room where you have lain since
they got you breathing again so we could be with you
when you died for the second time today.
Once you were gone male nurse kevin
shat out insincerities from the section
of the manual 'suggested phrases on the passing of loved ones'
each one thin and worn as the elbows
of an oxfam sweater and i don't doubt it must be hard
to know what to say kevin but no it wasn't
as if he held off dying till i got there
as if my father could perfectly estimate
the time it would take for me to get from
the house of fraser to find the car in the car park
i am sure i have parked in as if my father was somehow
able to factor in that i would join the motorway
in the wrong direction and go speeding north
when i should have gone speeding south
as if he could have timed so precisely
the traffic jam on the kingston bridge let alone
the parking nightmare that is wishaw hospital
at three o'clock on a tuesday when all the outpatients
are in you'll trust me won't you kevin
when i tell you i am not interested in your clichés
nor your supermarket custard creams fanned
out to look fancy on the plate. My father
died kevin forty-seven minutes after i arrived
and for every beat in the metronome of his slowing
song i counted his breaths in and fucking
out watched his adam's apple rise and fall

held his hand swallowed salt silently
screamed as entire cows and roofs and hairy
dogs called toto blustered through the eye
of my internal shit-storm if, kevin, my father
truly was waiting till i got there then surely
he would have died say sixty or ninety
seconds after my arrival or in the time
         it takes to boil an egg say four
         minutes tops—two if you want
         to dip soldiers in it.

let me eat cake and go quietly to seed

in this age of positive thinking
and mani-fucking-festation may i complain
proudly and publicly of ageing of all things
bodily may i wax lyrically of my now un-
obstructed bowel may i trumpet joyously
to the world of my failing eyes and drooping
breasts my liver spots and hearing loss
my increased cholesterol and hypertension
may i no longer feel obliged to appear
positive in the face of my increased
risk of heart disease may we stop calling
fucked-up situations 'challenges' and stop
looking for reasons bad things happen
there are none
may i never sport elastane cycling shorts
fluorescent orange jogging shoes
and t-shirts that urge the reader
to never never never give up
with the font size increasing like you are climbing
the arrochar alps one jagged peak at a time
may i never carry a water bottle—let me risk
dehydration from the house to the bus stop
how i am tired of counting my blessings
and watching my waistline please
just let me eat cake and go quietly
to seed may i continue to enjoy bearing
unnecessary grudges and curl up here
on the couch to watch christopher hitchens

denounce god on youtube may i climb
the paps of jura to sing my praises
across the monster-less loch of the breast
cancer i do not yet have and the ovaries
that once held hope may i tell of my gratitude
for the cervix that no longer needs to be papped
nor smeared, of my aching fingers and swollen
joints—how i can barely squeeze the sponge
into the corner of my loaf tin to dislodge
the baked on dough must i listen
to the woman on the train platform vomit her opinion
on refugees and the white teacher
talk of her surprise when the black kid
bled red must i worry the pains
in my chest at midnight mean i'm having
a heart attack must i tell the doctor my nails are softer
since she told me to stop eating cheese
must i now check the density of my bones
make appointments i cannot be bothered making
must they send me invitations to mammograms
and dental checks but never to champagne
and nibblies how i like to hear noise
how i like to make it how they take the eggs
from the battery hen but do not stop to hear
her song how i hear he is raping
his stepdaughter now how silence restricts
your wings how you never wanted to fly anyway.

iona i came from far

we were first at the please wait
here sign you with your back
to me the iona ferry just about visible
through the mist i came from far
to join you here we packed a picnic—
buttered rolls and mashed bananas
brown no doubt by the time we'd eat
them among the celtic crosses
and the thousand-year-old abbey
with its halogen downlights
and thermostatically controlled central
heating. November sun shines
where i've come from. The north
wind shrills here and i pace the frozen
silence between us photograph orange
crab baskets as they scuttle the shore
take secret shots of you looking out to sea
and far away from me a queue formed
behind you—christians mostly
sturdy walking shoes aran knit
jumpers bibles under their arms pilgrims
seeking their truths me with my camera
seeking mine.

the blue of god's fucking eyes

australia
         i see you
         differently now
         i am drifting
         my bags are packed
         i am trundling
backwards
         away from you
         on my own internal
         travelator you used
         to be enough
         your coconut dipped
         lamingtons your greasy
         chiko rolls your postcard
         fucking views your she'll
         be right
australia
         i am far from right
         i have aged
         what i thought i wanted
changed
         what i have is no longer
         enough a bald man
         in the street once told
         me it is an age thing
         someone else with hair
         arms flailing on a deserted
         beach under the hell

which is a january
sun roared to me above
an ocean so blue
like it was reflecting god's
own fucking eyes

how-can-this-not-be-enough?

    and i will
confess
    australia i do not know
    and i am not
alone
    sure the sydney blue gums
    feel it too we peel
    and shed in unison
    each of us attempting to
escape
    our own skins australia
    i leak in your searing
    heat i swim in pools
    of my own sweat
    and wake from menthol
    dreams of frosts and snow
    spread thick like wedding
    cake icing
i dream
    of winds that bite
    and howl up tenement closes—
    of back doors that slam shut
    with a reassuring bang

i have not heard here
of course i dream of other
things too twice this week
i broke my neck in dreams
the week before an old man
i met as i walked the dog
by the sea appeared
by my bed in a yellow
macintosh and matching
sou'wester
drenched
as though he'd just circum-
navigated the world's
oceans in an un-seaworthy
vessel single-handedly
he was bearing books
all of them dry australia
i cannot tell you
exactly what i am
looking
for all i can tell you is
it is
not here.

so she's not my friend and runs a fish & chip shop

specialising in greek mezze
and a dish called stifado
she finds out i write poems
tells me she could write one too it's easy
in between battering flatheads and twisting
potato strings around prawns i am encouraging
tell her she should go right ahead and write one
if it's that fucking easy i tell her i will read it not because
i am supportive but because i know it will be shit as if anyone
can write a poem without haemorrhaging internally
while reaching for the light and my friend who really
is my friend and a proper poet submits her internal bleeds
made external to competitions while i have only ever
sent my blood to pathology labs but never
to someone with the title of poetry judge
let me tell you how i see it

1. let me stand here with my poem in my hand

2. you stand there with your poem in your hand

3. let us ask someone (for example a complete stranger)

4. let us call this stranger marjory

5. let us ask marjory to tell us which poem she likes best

which one she deems worthy of the prize more often
than not mere cash dangled like an over-refrigerated
carrot at the tips of the noses of starving
poets let us watch those poets stampede
like a gaggle of gulls towards the solitary
french fry on the sand and isn't it like me holding
up a vanilla ice cream and my friend holding up a strawberry
ice cream and asking the ice cream vendor which flavour
he likes best? And isn't it like miss jean brodie asking
her girls who is the greatest italian painter—
and her girls replying 'leonardo da vinci miss'
and miss jean brodie replying: 'that is incorrect
—the answer is giotto, he is my favourite.'
And the woman who runs the fish & chip shop
advertises her dish called stifado as 'beef in a special'
which tells me nothing except that something is missing
like a miniature groom on a wedding cake standing beside
two fresh holes in the icing where his bride's stilettos
have been and the woman who's not my friend douses her
beef stifado as she douses everything in lemon and salt
and olive fucking oil and she thinks because
she loves her food that way
you should love it too.

o fair and gentle leek

then there was the okra dish
you made and the neighbours
who knocked on your door with
their christmas cheer you wouldn't let in
they'd brought a batch of cookies
they'd baked and decorated with silver
frosting and marzipan santas
this was the first time you'd
met them though you'd lived next
door for years you returned their
christmas cheer by telling them
you suffered panic attacks and
might on occasion have to knock
on their door in the middle of the night
you thought this was being neighbourly.
When you closed the door on them we sat
side by side at your too thin table
squashed hard up against the
back of your couch as though about
to eat a meal on a plane and the
guy in front does not have his chair
in the upright position. You'd
prepared okra—the traditional
egyptian way: boiled;
with tomatoes;
and too much lemon
and they are in season now
gracing the shelves of super-

markets the length of this
land and i know it is not their
intention to hurt; to remind of
what went before but i cannot
look them in the eye any more
cannot push my trolley down that
aisle cannot bear to see them
in all their fuzz and narcissism
laying alongside that fair and
gentle leek—her head turned
ever so slightly away pretending
her heart has not been broken
and then there is the internet
in all its stupidity who suggests
these okra taste of zucchini but to me
they will always taste of you.
And slime.
We ate shoulder to shoulder at your
too thin table in a kind of egyptian
economy class and you announced
with more than a little pride that
this was your signature dish, that
the acidity of the lemon was key
and i ate on—the intermittent silences
and citric acid causing old holes
in my gut to open up and scream for
me to run the truth is you soured
those okra with your too much lemon
like you soured everything with
your too much you.

my friend's vagina

i will not lie it is difficult not to wonder
what life will be like when you lose your job
and we have to move from this unaffordable
suburb by the sea i text my friend, though i should be writing
poetry—i gave up one day of salary
to do this. I call her my friend though our relationship
is a mere twelve months old, a *beaujolais nouveau*
if you will she has a dog called gypsy me a dog
called hector her husband has no kidneys
her varicose veins bulged—shone blue through her tight
    white pants
she had them removed—the veins not the pants i want to
    say publicly
but what i mean is on the public system
they went in through her groin. Some days after
the op i bumped into her in the supermarket.
She lifted her dress showed me the scar she was wearing
no knickers sent me a text later to thank me for letting
her show me her vagina in the supermarket
she is unperturbable a deep thinker an analyser
too much time on her hands in kidney wards she imagines
where else she might be—some weeks it's the back streets
of prague others the upper east side once upon a time
    shanghai
i tell her this constant living in her imagination
is her way of coping with a husband who has no kidneys
and a dialysis machine in the lounge room
that does not match the stag's head nor the map of africa

with the seychelles circled by her in black biro.
And she does not disagree. She is open to frankness
she is wise, sage-like the insight of a monk, she shaved
her head once. She is my go-to place when my mojo sags
when my full moon wanes when the feathers in my internal
doona need fluffing my text is frantic—but where will
we go if he loses his job and we have to move from this
unaffordable suburb by the sea? She would have been
in the kidney ward when my text arrived deep
in the turquoise ocean of her imagination, 'it doesn't
really matter where you go' she texted, 'the unhappiness
inside you will find you' and just as i'm thinking
maybe she'd shaved her head again
another text came through. 'In saying
that' she added, 'i've always rather
fancied acapulco'.

in praise of the fairy cake

(in the voice of Miss Jean Brodie)

19 February 2014

My Dearest Morag,

    It is with the deepest regret
I write to you now, to decline
your most gracious invitation,
to what i have no doubt will be the most
delectable of high teas—the many of which
I have so thoroughly enjoyed in the past.

    I had of course the fullest
intention of attending, indeed only
last night I was busy telling a dear
friend about it over the telephone,
before my father (without a great deal of notice
it has to be said) stopped breathing.
But make no mistake, Morag, I left no doubt
in my friend's mind as to my admiration
of your crustless egg and watercress,
your tinned red salmon and thinly sliced onion,
your Twinnings Earl Grey served in the bone china
teacups one can barely get a finger
through.

I only hope you can forgive
me, Morag, for this short notice and that you
will find it in yourself to understand the sadness
I feel, that besides your sandwiches,
neither will I be sampling your empire
biscuits, your millionaire's shortbread
nor your fairy cakes, the peaks of their little
wings so delicately dusted reminding
me of the freshly powdered peaks
of the Cuillins themselves.

In signing off, Morag, it is not beyond
the wildest imaginings that this high tea
will be yet another vibrant feather in your already
exquisite cap and I can only hope the gluten
free cup cakes you will no doubt have
bought in, for those with the stricter dietary
requirements, will not go uneaten.
My father will be buried on Saturday
morning, should you find yourself
at liberty to attend.

Your friend, sincerely and always,

Jean

in kuntry where sun is never stopping shining

my mother has sent me crystal doorknobs from scotland
that glisten in a way that knobs
do not glisten here. I will admit
they are not to everyone's taste. I remark
to the handyman who will fit my new knobs
upon the pity such knobs are not so readily
available here in australia he takes one
of them in his hand holds it up to the window
surveys the fractured shards of light that emanate
says personally he is not surprised they are not
for sale here. On opening the packet i discover
the metal rods required to connect the knobs
through the door panel are not included i must
now go to the hardware store where lower prices
are just the beginning i go to the lock aisle
i see from his name tag the lock man is called andrej
i tell andrej i am having new doors fitted that i already
have the knobs but i do not have the metal rod things
that connect them
'you already heff knobs but nothing to connect
them?' he asks as though such a thing were unimaginable
before adding, 'how many knobz you heff?'
'Sir, i have many knobs—indeed my knobs are a many
splendoured thing!' i say this thinking it may make andrej
laugh or at the very least smile i achieve neither
of these things he asks me too many door type
questions none of which i can answer

to his satisfaction he tells me in his kuntry
he is krime scene investigator that without
seeing my knobs he cannot tell me exactly
what i need
i tell him i will go to my car and get them
'pleez,' he says, 'go quvickly, already
i am finishing shift soon.' I race to my car.
I am mindful one minute over his finishing
time will most likely not be paid by the store
where lower prices are just the beginning.
I return.
Breathless.
Knobs in hand.
'How many doors?' he asks surveying the fractured
shards of light i tell him three he lifts his head
from the knobs and turns to face me 'can you say *three*
again pleez?' i roll my eyes—for the sake of finding
the metal rods for my knobs obediently i repeat
the word three.
'Ah, you are not from here!' he tells me raising
his index finger as though he just got one over on me
'you are pronouncing your Rs, here in auztralya
they are not pronouncing their Rs. VeRR you are from?
Eastern europe no?' i tell him i'm from scotland
that my grandparents were lithuanian that i'm asked daily
if i'm from poland. 'What about you andrej?'
Andrej tells me he is from ex-yugoslavia
and in the telling his face slides his eyelids lower
something of him disappears maybe back to the banks
of the danube or somewhere in sarajevo his expression
suspends as a spec of silver in colloid as though

his past just pressed pause on his present.
I wait.
Knobs in hand.
Allow him this space.
Eventually he comes back seems surprised
to see me standing in front of him in the middle
of the lock aisle in the store where lower prices
are just the beginning, 'auztralyan minister
for edukation should be ashamed!' he blurts out
'a kuntry charging van hundredt thousandT dollars
for degree!' then he glances over both his shoulders
looks me dead in the eye and whispers agitatedly,
'my kuntry, it vas socialist kuntry, do you understandt?'
and the urgency in his voice tells me it is of paramount
importance that i do, he clutches my forearm, 'edukation
vas free it vas vital ve hatt to educate our children
our health care vas free no one feared going to doktor
—when war came ve lost all of that,' and he does his best
to conceal the hairline fracture that's appearing
in his voice. 'One morning,' he said, rummaging
through lock type things on the shelf, 'i woke
and my city vas under siege, my neighbours
i drank tea with ver shooting each other dead i tried
to leave but i vas not allowed to.' He takes a packet
of lock type things from the shelf measures them against
the knobs puts it back and continues on his search
'in my kuntry i vas crime scene investigator,' he says,
'i vas essential to government thanks gott i did not have
to fight—any idiot vas handed gun and told to go shoot
people dead.' He pulls out another lock type thing
from the shelf measures it against the knobs puts it back

'my vife, she got out—she took the children they vent to malta
i did not see them for thirty-nine months.'
Eventually andrej was reunited with them
then they fled here to australia and he is grateful
for the peace that fills his days here though
'the people here, they do not vant to know
about rest of vorld,' he says,
'all they vant to talk about is how this is best kuntry
in vorld, how great is beaches, how their sun is never
stopping shining.' He continues rummaging through his shelves.
'This war,' he says 'is keeping me awake in the night,'
and i can see it is keeping him awake in the day
it took more than twenty minutes till andrej was satisfied
he had the correct metal rod things for my knobs
and i do not know if the store where lower prices
are just the beginning would have paid him the extra
and i do not think he would have cared
after the thorough search one would expect
from a crime scene investigator andrej handed
me three of the exact metal rod things my knobs required
removed his working mitt took my hand and held it
and i saw the fractured shards of his light
do their best to glisten in a country where people
do not want to know about the rest of the world
where sun is never stopping shining and where the minister
for education should be ashamed charging one hundred
thousand dollars for degree and i felt sheepish
to have marched in there with my first world problems
and crystal knobs which certainly were a many splendoured
thing but i left the store richer that day and learnt
much, the very least of which was the word spindle.

when the eagles have finished
taking it easy

and john denver

has filled up our senses like sleepy

blue oceans i will stand at the chapel door

allow mourners to say what they think they should

say shake hands with faces i do not recognise drink a

cup of stewed tea inhale a dry scone accept the solitary

sympathy card from your best friend's daughter ring

my brother who has chosen not to come re-read the

note your sort-of wife has had printed on your order

of service urging mourners to not waste money

on perfumed wreaths that might comfort

you on your way but rather to give

generously to a disease you

didn't even know you

had.

this is a prayer for the soul of my boy

it happened on a thursday
he was big, brown, a dog,
sixty-five kilos nearly
ten years old frisky on occasion
but mostly he was placid
we went everywhere together
hung out in cafes his velvet brown eyes
lined thick with black kohl perfect
for extricating left over sausages and buttered
crusts from the unlikeliest of donors
and there were some who'd say but he looks so sad!
and i'd say—do not be fooled! it is merely
his eyeliner—and an insatiable appetite for sausages
and i'm not saying he never felt sad, his brother
died two weeks before he did, i often wonder if he knew
he loved things like pizza and bacon
he was gentle with manners—it was like angels
lived in him he slept on his trampoline
raised up from the floor to ward off arthritis
it did nothing for tumours i left him once to go to scotland
returned three weeks later woke groggy from jet lag
he was sitting by my bed leaning in—his head pushed
hard up against my pillow staring unflinchingly
with the same dedication he might give to a slice of pepperoni
and mozzarella. After he died a woman on the beach
gave me a photograph she'd taken of him and me together
we are sitting on the sand side by side staring
out beyond the breakers we look like we are inseparable

every day of the too few years we had him devotion
coursed from him i was his master the keeper of sausages
the caller of walkies the turner of blind eyes
when he'd jump up and steal expensive chunks of camembert
and sticky date puddings from christmas
tables we always knew we'd only ever have him till he reached
around ten these giant boys do not last near long enough—
something about their bones their joints malignant
tumours if we were lucky he'd have the slow growing
kind it was two in the morning
the vet's surgery was next door to the train station
as though planned that way so that when it was over
freight trains might come in the night
for the cargos of pain from hearts so broken
they might never recover
we stepped out of the surgery into the inconceivable
night the grief train in our name rumbled
in and halted with the same certainty
as death and we piled its wagons
high with great shovels of our grief
then we stood back—exhausted
sweat on our brows warm shovels in our hands we were emptied
and this was only the start of it.

single ply toilet paper

           i think i liked things better
           when you were checking yourself into emergency
departments with panic attacks
brought on, you said, from being too far away from me
i even preferred things when you thought you had bladder
cancer with weeks to live
we grew close those seven days you washed
my clothes for me referred to the other side
of your bed as mine ordered the sizzling tofu
ahead of my arrival at the lucky red dragon
on the main street it was january
we found a cottage by the sea spent four days
there together shopped at the grocery store in the village
you carried the basket with one hand held mine
with the other bought irish soda scones
long life soya milk single ply toilet paper if your tumour
cleared up you were leaving for cairo in february—
eight months of filming in the sahara you asked
if i would join you and i said yes and after cairo
you'd be leaving for LA—two months of filming
in the mojave and you asked if i would join
you and i said yes and when your tumour disappeared
and you prepared to leave for cairo without
me i will not lie it was difficult
to wish you well in fact i wished you'd die horribly
say in a light plane crash in the sahara
or by gunshot wound in LA and the ship carrying
your equipment and six months of supplies

would sink tragically off the costa de la muerte
where your long life soy milk would spoil your single
ply toilet paper turn to mush and shoals of gilt headed
bream would swim curiously through your pile of drowning
camera parts and glance briefly into your lens before
darting in the opposite direction
as fast as their fins could carry them.

duty free fags

and after he died
they/people/customers of mine
said how strange
to have been there
like it was meant to be
that i would touch down
in glasgow
at that precise time
and it was like they were saying
the universe
or god
or some
thing
had planned it this way
and i said to them
i also came home three
years ago i saw lochs the colour
of a dulux sample card crossed
the sound of sleat to the isle of skye
ate cullen skink at cafe gandolfi
and nobody died
nor the time before
when andrew and i hiked
through the fairy glen
lost our footing and tumbled
down the old man of storr
carving a trench with our arses
we landed in a heap one

on top of the other
astonishing sheep laughed
so hard i turned the snow
yellow around us
and i have not many kin
left in scotland now
and it is not that they have died
we have merely drifted
as snow might drift on rannoch moor
in the thick of winter januaries
time will do this
and distance
and these days i do not forewarn
with airline itineraries
nor details of stopovers in exotic locations
i keep secret
my timing of tumbles
and cullen skinks
that i might save my kin
the wringing of hands and pacing of midnight floors
that they may remain
blissfully unaware
of my arrival into glasgow
with my duty free fags
and my kiss of death.

a lake full of fucking swans

it's been twenty years now i am finally
adopting their tongue i now refer
to renovations as renos when nothing's
a problem i say no worries if i want
to meet someone in the afternoon
i refer to that time of day after
morning but before nightfall as arvo
but i will not cook my tenderloins
in their great outdoors will not drape
myself in their flag on the twenty-sixth
of january will not take part
in the excitement of their meat
raffles on a friday night and i do not disagree
their oceans are pretty—but i am not interested
in pretty where i come from the sea
is a dark and troubled thing that whips
up winds that howl me home and leave
the taste of salt and blood and life
in me i have never stepped in their oceans
but i have hiked through their bush
i have pondered their landscapes
and it is not that they do not speak
to me it is just that they do not sing. The lady
with the eighties hair tells me the swimsuit
i've chosen is too old for me
i have decided on the one with the little skirt
it will save me waxing my bikini
line at this age i have enough

to do she hears my accent asks me where i'm from how long
i've been here like she's interviewing
me and will later be handing my responses
to the department of immigration
i tell her i'm from scotland
i've been here for twenty years
that i've yet to own a swimsuit here
twenty years and never owned a swimsuit she says
then asks why i haven't integrated
into their way of life yet and the intonation
goes up at the end it is how they speak here
then the racist with the eighties
hair suggests the high-cut leg
i try it on to show her i am grateful that i am open
to suggestion that i will do as i am told
the only mirror sits in the middle of the store
packed with fully clothed shoppers i plod
semi naked towards it with great dollops
of shame i squint at my reflection i look like i am wearing
a borat mankini. The racist with the eighties hair
and the over-pencilled eyebrows tells me the high-cut
swimsuit makes my legs look longer
i do not tell her i am fine with their current
length. My sister scattered my father's ashes
on lake windermere
lake windermere is in england the celebrant
said my father liked it very much there—apparently
he also liked california once upon a time
he liked places like girvan pier the falls
of clyde the mull of kintyre the ailsa craig
and now he is floating in england

on a lake full of fucking swans.
I ended up buying the swimsuit with the little
skirt i feel it is important to make your own decisions
in life whether it be about waxing your bikini
line or cooking your free range chicken breasts
in their great outdoors and i wonder what decisions
he'd have made knowing his final trip away
from scotland would have been in an urn
in the back seat of the car and would have lasted
for all eternity when so often the best bit about
going away is heeding the howl
of the wind and coming home.

on making a chocolate cake and not fucking up what's left of your relationship

first you must peak the egg whites but before
that you must melt the chocolate the chocolate
must be of good quality if you are making
a chocolate mousse but if it is just a sponge cake
coles' cooking chocolate is good enough
you can buy it in the baking aisle
then you must melt the chocolate in a stainless
steel bowl over a pot of hot water
you must not get any water in the chocolate
if you get water in the chocolate you must google
to see what to do next when you go to mix
all the ingredients together you will discover
you do not have the baking powder
you were sure you had you must
then go to coles and park on the street
it is quicker than the car park
once in coles you will not be able to remember
if you require baking powder or bicarbonate
of soda they appear to be the same thing to you
you will deliberate extensively
buy a packet of each stay longer than the thirty
minute parking spot return home with a parking
fine you must now look for the round cake
tin you are sure you had for fuckssake
you made a fucking cake at christmas
time you take out the oblong roasting

tin that's not quite deep enough it has traces
of roast lamb and a rosemary sprig in the corner
you rinse it out pour your cake mixture in
this will be the third cake you have ever
made the first was a crumble in the blue mountains
you made it from wild rhubarb and crab apples
from the mad woman at work's orchard
she also brought greengages one day gooseberries another
they were sour and hairy they reminded
you of your youth you poached the rhubarb
and the crab apples, you did not add sugar,
you crumbled flour and butter added oats for fibre
and general health you set it under
the grill instead of the oven the oats
caught fire your relationship was breaking
down you had met and fallen in love with another
man who suffered a certain degree
of narcissism and borderline personality
disorder you tried not to be too hard on yourself
though you experienced considerable
pain in your heart region your husband attempted
suicide you turn the oven knob to ON
the grill element turns red but the oven
does not come on you remember
the knob fell off the day of the roast
lamb you stuck it back on in the wrong position
you must now turn the knob to 'grill'
if you want the fucking oven to come on
the LED clock flashes continuously
in green yes you fucking know
you need to set the clock before the timer

will work you lay down your oblong roasting
tin count to ten light a scented candle
run a bath with the pine salts you bought at coles
try to imagine the stone cottage in the field filled
with sunflowers or lavender or maybe it was roses
you clench a pencil between
your teeth stare at the sun till you sneeze
next week you will attempt a victoria sponge
perhaps even a chocolate and beetroot
cake you got the recipe from the mad woman
at work who brings the crab apples the rhubarb
the greengages sometimes so ripe
even the birds won't eat them.

and my heart crumples like a coke can

you never ate fusilli nor farfalle nor spaghettini. you did not like all that italian shite. you liked chocolate eclairs penguin biscuits beef with string in gravy and custard with steamed pudding which is like a fruit cake. a long time ago we wished you would die. you loved tractors and bob-cats. a bob-cat is the australian name for a digger. one winter you dug a hole in a field with your bob-cat cut off the electricity supply to the entire village burst the mains water pipe. the water froze children skated on it wayward cars skidded into badgers and lambs born in unseasonal snow. your father was a farmer. he gave you your love of tractors. and potatoes. he skimped on other sorts of love. once you gifted a plough to mum. and a socket set. another time a cement mixer. you smoked and drank. grouse mostly. embassy regals. one time you moved a washing machine for a neighbour. you bought old tractors and renovated them sold them in the classifieds. although you could not spell it you were an entrepreneur. your legs went thin. the nutritionist said all you had to do was drink complan. you used to wash your car a lot. the celebrant at your funeral said you would be on your way to heaven in a gleaming vehicle. nobody laughed. you were not religious. i do not believe in heaven. your brother in canada rings me a lot since you died. he told me you were coeliac. it is unrelated to motor neurone disease. you were seventy fucking two. david bowie sixty-nine. alan rickman the same. your adam's apple stopped moving. i realise i too will stop breathing one day. at your funeral your sort-of-wife asked for donations to the disease you didn't know you had. i don't know if anyone donated. nine days before you died i visited you at your pebble dashed house sat beside you on your tan leather couch watched upside down chaffinches feed on the bird nuts hanging from the hills hoist in your front garden. a hills hoist is australian. in scotland it is a whirly jig. i have been away too long. you tried to make your way to the bathroom on your zimmer frame. you fell in the hallway. i didn't know how to get you up. i lay beside you on the carpet. you kept apologising. there was nothing to apologise for. the nutritionist was wrong. you died the tuesday after valentine's day. valentine's day was on the friday. stephen hawking had motor neurone disease too. his was different to the kind you had. there are four different kinds. yours was diagnosed the day you died. you were already dead. stephen hawking liked cosmological stuff and the big bang. you liked tractors. when i think of how much you liked tractors, my heart crumples like a coke can.

the reason your phone is not ringing

is because it does not occur to him to dial your number.
There will be times you will think this is because
his angular heart lies like a pile of un-put together
lego bricks and hearing your voice might bring back
the longing in him
there will be times when even you will roll your eyes
at this suggestion
many months will pass you will display typical
and atypical symptoms of a heart that is no longer
merely wounded but now infected you will get a dog
the dog will help greatly with the infection
though your wound will weep longer
than even you would have expected
you will go to scotland for a holiday
the change of air will do you good
while you are there your father will die
you will fly back to australia the morning
after you bury him two months later you will sell
your house and buy another
four years will pass
your marriage will improve but your dog will die
one day the cause of your infection will find himself in a
    supermarket
he will see a pile of single ply toilet paper on special
you will pop into his head like a 5 watt
light bulb just illuminated a corner of his mind
where the sun don't shine which is to say all of his mind
he will dial your number and leave you a voicemail

the best part about this voicemail will be at first
you do not recognise who it is you will replay
the voicemail three times before your penny will drop
when your penny drops your skin will momentarily crawl
and he will tell you he only thought of you because
he saw the single ply toilet paper on special
even he will sound surprised you popped into his head
interestingly you will not feel sad the single
ply toilet paper reminded him of you
this non-sad feeling will indicate your infection is finally
coming under control and you may now reduce
your dressing changes to once per day though
you must continue to keep them covered
whilst showering you will momentarily wonder
how you could ever have been attracted
to someone who thinks of you when he sees single ply toilet
paper you will then remember this is consistent
you will replay the bit at the end of the voicemail
where he says call me back if you're up for it
the best bit will be you are not up for it
you now get to be the one who is not doing
the calling back you will feel no shame
in admitting you enjoy this feeling very much your marriage
will continue to improve you will remember
your dog with great fondness you will keep his collar
and stainless steel water bowl under the driver's
seat of your car when you go over a bump you will hear
the clink of his name tag against his water bowl
you are not ready to let him go yet.

hector my hector

and the way he stared
you know
at the deck
like a wax works dummy
what i mean is in the shade
without the sun on his face
how he looked a beiged jaundice and how
colour consultants might call that taupe
and how i have not the head for contemporary shades
the teals
the corals
the terracottas—i like things plain
i like for brown to be brown and beige
to be beige i understand
when someone tells me
something is blue but what i'm saying
is he was the colour of a mannequin
that nude taupeness—
grief strained through skin
and how i put the kettle on though neither of us would eat
    till the tuesday
and the way he stared
you know, at the deck
and how
grief coursed from him how it took the colour
from his eyes
the adjectives from his mouth
and how it broke through

his knees his fingers
practically his ankles
and how it poured down through
the holes in the deck onto the steps
of our neighbours below
and how they wouldn't have minded they've had dogs
    themselves
and how you feel you'll never
recover
like, ever
and how coming home is the worst—
how he'd bring us a shoe
sometimes a pair; a rolled up
newspaper; a plastic tiramisu
container each groove licked to
infinity and how he would
wag his tail that hard against
the walls our neighbours would hear it
and how they wouldn't have minded they've had dogs
    themselves
and how in his excitement his ears
would twist and flick forwards
like the handlebars of a racer
and how that was his way of saying
i am so fucking happy right now
i think i might explode.

the shit we are in

no more no less than anyone
else we found this guy couples' therapist
tri-level terrace
paddington
handy
for coffee afterwards
in one of those groovy
cafes he came down to the waiting
room to meet us says ali and john?
i say ali and *thomas*
ah! he says are we here to talk about
someone called john and snickered
wheezily like muttley from whacky races
we rolled our eyes followed him to his office.
He was italian, reminded us of a toad
with his facial warts, swollen throat
mouth a horizontal line like kermit
and yes i have been known to confuse my amphibians
he tells us he listens to his patients seventy
per cent of the time the other thirty he said he'd be thinking
'bout other things like dinner, his girlfriend ballroom dancing
and when he wasn't thinking 'bout dinner, his girlfriend
ballroom dancing he made us sit in chairs opposite
each other like porcelain figurines instructed
us to hold hands look into each others eyes
and take the whole fucking thing seriously
his fee was three hundred and twenty dollars
thomas rustled chewing gum packets clicked

his pen incessantly i threw him daggers he could not see he is
    legally blind
and while we sat opposite
each other like porcelain figurines
we had to say shit like:
thomas last week when i asked you to clean
the leek for soup and you didn't do it i was hurt
then thomas was meant to say shit like: i'm sorry
i hurt you it was unkind of me to promise
to clean the leek and then not do it
only by this time thomas and i are both laughing
our tits off because
it's *absurd*
then the toad tells us if we think it's funny
then how 'bout this is the last session
only he was raging
you could tell by the way his throat ballooned
in and out so we said fine
paid our bill left walked towards
oxford street to the groovy cafes united
in our did-we-just-get-fired-from-therapy
sort of outrage we held hands voluntarily the sun was setting
it was a gentle night
heat had seared all day
the man on the news said someone
out west fried an egg on a shovel
and then this breeze came from somewhere
bondi maybe clovelly wrapped itself
around us we stopped under a street lamp snogged
unexpectedly he lit a gitanes girls with legs skinny
as spaghetti in jeans walked past in all honesty

we are nowhere near groovy enough
for this town we found a cafe dimly
lit tucked ourselves in ordered our decafs—caffeine
and proximity to bedtime is an equation we simply
must consider these days
the waiter with the garland of roses in his hair
delivered the decafs we sipped on them
thomas said sorry 'bout the leek
i said don't worry about it it's just a fucking leek
and scraped the chocolaty froth from inside my cup
then we headed to the car thomas lit another fag
mind if i smoke in the car? he asked
knock yourself out i said
he rolled down the windows
turned on the air the car filled
and swirled in thick blue smoke as we drove into
the night and never looked back.

dead man farting

how some people will think it's disrespectful
to talk about his farting now he's not here
how mum and i drove through the snow followed
the river took the sharp left turn up the hill
to his pebble dashed house where he lay on his back
on his tan leather couch his sort-of-wife
handed us coffee we did not want bowls of home-made
ice cream we could not eat. Sure ice cream
is for birthday cakes and yuletide logs and single nougats
on day trips to largs at the glasgow fair not made on doctor's
orders with mars bars and double cream and too much sugar
to build up the limbs of a man once solid and un-splittable
as a scottish elm sure when ice cream comes on prescription
it is no longer ice cream but a bowl of calories for a dying man
i held the coffee cup in one hand the bowl of ice cream
in the other they were things i could hold onto—objects
that filled the space in the silence that comes
when there is nothing left to say. Then he pierced
the quiet faintly whispered how he needed to break his gas
how i had never heard it put like that before how i am familiar
with the breaking of wind the passing of gas indeed
the humble fart and then he groaned
rolled onto his side with his rice noodle arm poking
out from under his blanket like a trafficator
on an old ford while he scrambled from his couch
like a novice mountaineer attempting to scale the heights
of ben nagar in a thick pea souper without an ice pick
or walking poles or fucking gaiters

and there was nothing to his legs—no bulk no substance
they jerked up and down at the knee as though obeying
the commands of an unseen puppeteer and the too thin
skin on his shrunken pins hung sad like loosely pegged
washing on a breezeless glasgow green
once on his feet he grabbed onto his zimmer
dragged himself across what may as well have been the length
of the arctic tundra out into the hall where he closed
the door behind himself and he broke his gas
only we could all hear it and it seemed strange
to have gone to all that effort then not try to keep
it quiet then the door burst open he clattered
back in and millimetred his way back across the shag pile
of his tundra to his tan leather couch fell backwards
into it exhaling loudly part exhaustion part satisfaction
and mouthed the words 'i'm sorry'.
It's been more than two years since he died
and i don't think back to fatherly things we did together
he wasn't the fatherly kind of guy and it's not really
the fart i think back to either—mostly it's the apology
how i think it was his way of proudly showing
us how hard he'd worked on his manners
since mum left him how he was now a man
of the new millennium—a man who topped up sweet sherries
before his own whisky glass a man who asked
are you sure you won't be cold when you stepped
out into the winter snow a man who now forewarned
and apologised for breaking his gas
the night before he died his lungs more colander
than sponge struggled to hold on to air and he breathed
the terrified breath of a sparrow rescued

from the clutches of the neighbour's cat
and kept in a shoebox with holes stabbed
in the lid for oxygen and light and somehow
that night my father managed to knit and purl
enough words together—whispery as though his throat
were lined with feathers—to tell mum the last ten years
without her had been the worst of his life.
He up and left this world the following
day and i imagine this man of the new millennium
who now forewarned of threatening winds and unashamedly
told of his feelings left him all the freer to go
and i don't think he'd have minded one bit me talking
about his farting like this sure my dead father
enjoyed a good fart story as much
as the next dead guy.

if you write poetry but do not like conversation

what you can do is you can tell people at parties
that you write poetry and what that means is the people
at the parties will not know what to say to you
if they do say something mostly it will be that they do not
    like poetry
but because you are at a party you must make conversation
so you will say to them to not like poetry is to say
you do not like one of your ears or your right kidney
or seeing the frost curl and rise at dawn to lick the
    world silver
sometimes when you tell people you write poetry
what they will understand is that you stare out of the window
for too many hours and wear a cravat and smoke cigarettes
in a long cigarette holder and that you do not do anything
of any real value because you do not earn any money
from doing this thing what they will also understand
is because you write poetry you must be a poet
but they will not understand the act of writing
poetry does not necessarily make you a poet
if you try to explain this to them they will have to excuse
themselves and go to the kitchen to top up their sparkling
lambruscos because they think it is champagne
then the next person who comes will also ask you
what you do and you will say the poetry thing again
and they will ask you why you write poetry
and you will say because scottish heather flourishes
in the harshest of spots like the cracks of rocks

where there's no love and still it survives
and they will not know what you are talking
about and will think that sometimes you wear smocks
and puffy sleeves and only ever write things about tulip
petals and emerald fields and newborn lambs, etc.
and sometimes they will ask you how long it takes
to write a poem and you will tell them one week or fifty-
two it depends and the waiter will come around
with the platter of vol-au-vents and the blinis
topped with smoked salmon and an inch of crème fraîche
with the sprig of green dill planted like a baby christmas
tree knee deep in snow and this will be the perfect moment
for them to move away to the kitchen and top up their
sparklings too and finally you will be left alone only
you are never really alone because you will always
have your bag filled with the notebooks and the backs
of napkins and the gaggles of pens and when the party
is over your notes will say things like—

   1. *google blini ingredients*
   2. *sparkling lambrusco is not champagne*
   3. *writing poetry does not make you a poet any more*
      than not killing an ant will make you a buddhist

and you will be satisfied you went to the party
and that you tried to make conversation but you decide
you will not go to the parties of the future
and you will not hate the people for not loving
poetry in the way that you love it
sure there was a time you hated poetry too.

end matters

For the record, I'd like to publicly acknowledge that I have never drunk, nor do I ever intend to drink, Coke. Except that one time, on holiday in Spain when the man with the egg-shaped head poking through his hair like Mount Kosciuszko rising up through the clouds brought me a glass of something black and fizzy as I lay by the pool frying my limbs in coconut oil, like chicken tenderloins in a teflon pan. 'Grouse and Coke?' he asked, handing me the glass. I took off my sunglasses, which were already sliding down the bridge of my nose on account of the oil, looked him dead in the eye, part disbelief part disgust and said, 'Grouse . . . and fucking Coke?' Grouse and Irn Bru I could have coped with—but Grouse and Coke, I'm sorry, was a carbonated beverage too far. Naturally, on account of me not wanting to appear rude, I drank it down immediately. Sure, if we hadn't cremated him, my father would have turned in his Grouse-sodden grave.

acknowledgements

I am indebted to Kevin MacNeil who, in the middle of a hectic book tour and performances and teaching and reading from his magnificent *The Brilliant & Forever*, still found time to look at my work and run through it with me on Skype. Thank you, Kevin, for your eyes sharp as a brand new Bic disposable razor and for your overwhelming support and generosity that went above and beyond as I buffed these poems into the best versions of themselves.

Charles Bukowski, whose '*grasping at the curtains like a drunken monk and tearing them down, down, down*', set me free as a writer in ways I could never have imagined.

My mum who is always there with an international bank transfer, a screwdriver, an electric drill and a twenty-litre pot of scotch broth you could stand a spoon in and who, despite her own fear of massive tarantulas, took the cardboard box the fridge came in, held it up towards the tarantula on the wall, imagining he'd simply jump inside and wait patiently, while she ran outside to release him into the bush.

My sister, whose tears were the barometer that told me a poem was good enough.

My brother (the King of Scotland) and Fiona (the Snow Queen) for the song they wrote for me so long ago. Its words and melody buoy me still. It sings to me daily as I write.

My niece Alexandra, whose existence made me see the world in ways I didn't know were possible.

My non-friend Bron Coleman, artist and writer who, when all's said and done, is more sister than friend and has encouraged me since these poems were mere scraps in the unswept corners of my mind.

My friend and poet Kerryn Valeontis for the celery on the lawn, the foetal position, the guacamole and the laughter that would so often turn to howling.

My friend Karen who just seems to understand everything and whose vagina proudly features in one of these poems.

Kri, who thrust these poems into the hands of better poets around town and brought me feedback that made me feel proud.

My editor, Julia Beaven, for waltzing wholeheartedly with these poems from day one. The kind of editor one imagines could only exist in dreams.

Wakefield Press. Who just feel like family.

And Hector, we couldn't have loved him more.

Wakefield Press is an independent publishing and
distribution company based in Adelaide, South Australia.
We love good stories and publish beautiful books.
To see our full range of books, please visit our website at
wakefieldpress.com.au
where all titles are available for purchase.
To keep up with our latest releases, news and events,
subscribe to our monthly newsletter.

Find us!

Facebook: facebook.com/wakefield.press
Twitter: twitter.com/wakefieldpress
Instagram: instagram.com/wakefieldpress